NOTES

NOTES

Study the Word in a Year

Old Testament Questions and Answers

by

Joseph L. Avery, Jr.

ARPress

ILLUMINATING IDEAS
EMPOWERING VOICES

ARPress
45 Dan Road Suite 5
Canton MA 02021
Hotline: 1(888) 821-0229
Fax: 1(508) 545-7580

Ordering Information:
Quantity sales. Special discounts are available on quantity purchases by corporations, associations, and others. For details, contact the publisher at the address above.

Printed in the United States of America.

ISBN-13:   Softcover   979-8-89676-251-5

                  eBook   979-8-89676-252-2

Library of Congress Control Number: 2025904627

Honor Pastor Isaiah Avery.

NOTES

Genesis

- What are the two great lights? Chapter 1
- How did man become a living soul? Chapter 2
- What is cursed above all cattle? Chapter 3
- What was crieth unto the Lord? Chapter 4
- Who walked with God? Chapter 5
- What did God repent of? Chapter 6
- Who shuts the ark? Chapter 7
- What is in man's heart since his youth? Chapter 8
- What is the covenant between God and Noah? Chapter 9
- What sons divided the earth? Chapter 10
- What was the reason God dividing the language? Chapter 11
- What covenant did God make with Abram? Chapter 12
- What men were wicked and sinners before the Lord? Chapter 13
- Who gave tithes of all? Chapter 14
- What was counted for righteousness? Chapter 15
- Who will be a wild man? Chapter 16
- What does Abraham mean? Chapter 17
- Who laughed and lied? Chapter 18
- Who was blinded? Chapter 19

- Why did God close the womb of Abimelech's wife? Chapter 20
- For which son did Abraham make a feast? Chapter 21
- Who went to the land of Moriah? Chapter 22
- Why did Abraham purchase the burying place? Chapter 23
- Who is the Damsel? Chapter 24
- Who are the two nations in Rebekah's womb? Chapter 25
- Who was fair to look upon? Chapter 26
- How did Jacob steal the blessing from his brother? Chapter 27
- What was the name of the house of God? Chapter 28
- How many years did Jacob labor when he married the firstborn? Chapter 29
- How many wives did Jacob have? Chapter 30
- What did Rachel do to Laban? Chapter 31
- What was the name of the place where Jacob saw God face-to-face? Chapter 32
- Who is Elelohe-Israel? Chapter 33
- What happened to Jacob's daughter? Chapter 34
- What sin did Reuben commit? Chapter 35
- Who is Edom? Chapter 36
- Why was Joseph hated by his brothers? Chapter 37
- What shame did Judah do? Chapter 38
- Why did Joseph go to the prison? Chapter 39
- Who did not remember Joseph? Chapter 40
- Why did Joseph get released from jail? Chapter 41

- What was required to release Simeon? Chapter 42
- What was an abomination? Chapter 43
- Who is the lad? Chapter 44
- Why did Benjamin receive more raiment than the other brothers? Chapter 45
- Why did Jacob go to Egypt? Chapter 46
- Where was Israel buried? Chapter 47
- Where was Rachael buried? Chapter 48
- Where was the burial place located? Chapter 49
- Why did fear come upon Joseph's brothers? Chapter 50

Exodus

- What were the midwives ordered to do? Chapter 1
- What does "Moses" mean? Chapter 2
- What was God's name? Chapter 3
- What signs show the presence of God? Chapter 4
- What evil entreated the children of Israel? Chapter 5
- What name was not known to Jacob? Chapter 6
- Was Moses a god? Chapter 7
- How many swarms of flies remained? Chapter 8
- How many cattle of Israel died? Chapter 9
- What did Moses promise Pharaoh? Chapter 10
- What was God's last plague? Chapter 11
- What was the purpose for the blood? Chapter 12
- What happened to Joseph's bones? Chapter 13
- How did the sea divide? Chapter 14
- Who is the man of war? Chapter 15
- What did the people do on the seventh day? Chapter 16
- What did Moses write in the book? Chapter 17
- What was the thing that Moses did that was not good? Chapter 18
- What will happen if you keep "my covenant"? Chapter 19

- Why did the people want Moses to speak to them and not God? Chapter 20
- What was the judgment for a life? Chapter 21
- What flesh can you not eat? Chapter 22
- What are the three national feasts? Chapter 23
- Who was Moses' minister? Chapter 24
- What was in the ark? Chapter 25
- What divided the holy place and the most holy place? Chapter 26
- What caused the lamp to burn always? Chapter 27
- What shall be on his forehead? Chapter 28
- What is a sweet savor offering? Chapter 29
- What was the condition to avoid death? Chapter 30
- What was the condition to avoid death? Chapter 31
- Who repented? Chapter 32
- What will happen if you see the Lord's face? Chapter 33
- Who is jealous? Chapter 34
- What kind of heart for giving? Chapter 35
- What did Moses command the people to do? Chapter 36
- What five items were made with gold? Chapter 37
- What two items were made with silver? Chapter 38
- What was the writing on the crown? Chapter 39
- What signs were given for the journey? Chapter 40

Leviticus

- What was required to make atonement? Chapter 1
- What season was required for the meat offering? Chapter 2
- The fat and blood belong to whom? Chapter 3
- How many times does the priest sprinkle the blood? Chapter 4
- What is a trespass offering? Chapter 5
- What cannot be eaten? Chapter 6
- What is a peace-offering? Chapter 7
- What was applied to sanctify Aaron? Chapter 8
- Why did the people shout? Chapter 9
- What will bring death to Aaron and his sons? Chapter 10
- What things in the water can you eat? Chapter 11
- How many days to be circumcised? Chapter 12
- How long shall he dwell alone? Chapter 13
- What was used for atonement? Chapter 14
- Before entering in the tabernacle, you must be what? Chapter 15
- What was used for atonement? Chapter 16
- What is the life of the flesh? Chapter 17
- Who shall not lie with mankind? Chapter 18
- What is a print? Chapter 19
- Who was separated from other people? Chapter 20

- Who shall be burnt with fire? Chapter 21
- What is a blemish offering? Chapter 22
- How many feasts are there of Jehovah? Chapter 23
- What will happen if you blasphemy Lord? Chapter 24
- Who are the Lord's servants? Chapter 25
- As long as the land is desolate it will enjoy her...? Chapter 26
- All tithes belong to whom? Chapter 27

Numbers

- From twenty years old and upward, to where were you able to go? Chapter 1
- What tribe was not numbered? Chapter 2
- What tribe was charged to do the service of the tabernacle? Chapter 3
- How many were numbered to do the service in the tabernacle? Chapter 4
- What is a jealousy offering? Chapter 5
- What is the law of the Nazarite? Chapter 6
- What was the dedication to the altar? Chapter 7
- At what age do they stop serving the tabernacle? Chapter 8
- What must be kept in its appointed season? Chapter 9
- When did they blow without an alarm? Chapter 10
- How many elders were chosen for Moses? Chapter 11
- Why did Miriam receive leprous? Chapter 12
- What man wanted to possess the land? Chapter 13
- How many times did they tempt the Lord? Chapter 14
- What is a drink-offering? Chapter 15
- Who have not done anything with their own mind? Chapter 16
- How many rods were there? Chapter 17

- What is a wave-offering? Chapter 18
- What was the law of the ordinances? Chapter 19
- How did the water come out of the rock? Chapter 20
- Who died from the serpents? Chapter 21
- Why did the ass go another way? Chapter 22
- Who is Balaam? Chapter 23
- Why was Balak angry? Chapter 24
- How many died in the plague? Chapter 25
- How many men were there after the wilderness? Chapter 26
- Who replaced Moses? Chapter 27
- When is the Passover of the Lord? Chapter 28
- When is the holy convocation? Chapter 29
- What is a vow? Chapter 30
- Why was there a plague among the children of Israel? Chapter 31
- What happened to those men from twenty years old and upward? Chapter 32
- Who died in Mount Hor? Chapter 33
- What land shall fall unto you for an inheritance? Chapter 34
- How many cities are used for refuge? Chapter 35
- Who can the daughters of Zelophehad marry? Chapter 36

Deuteronomy

- Who does not have knowledge between good and evil? Chapter 1
- What people were called the land of giants? Chapter 2
- Who did God command to inherit the land? Chapter 3
- Who is a consuming fire? Chapter 4
- What is needed to prolong your days in the land which ye shall possess? Chapter 5
- What is the commandment? Chapter 6
- Why did the Lord choose you? Chapter 7
- Who giveth power to get wealth? Chapter 8
- Who did not eat for forty days and forty nights? Chapter 9
- Who was made to be multitude as the stars of heaven? Chapter 10
- I set before you this day a blessing and a...? Chapter 11
- Forsake not what tribe as long as thou livest? Chapter 12
- What sign shows you are a true prophet? Chapter 13
- The Lord has chosen thee to be what kind of people? Chapter 14
- Pour what upon the ground as water? Chapter 15

- What does the Lord thy God hateth? Chapter 16
- How many witnesses needed to be put to death? Chapter 17
- Who is the Lord's inheritance? Chapter 18
- All thine eyes shall not pity what? Chapter 19
- Why can you cut the trees in the field? Chapter 20
- What was the law for a stubborn and rebellious son? Chapter 21
- What is an abomination unto the Lord? Chapter 22
- Whatever thou hast promised with thy mouth, thou shalt what? Chapter 23
- What is the rule for a new wife? Chapter 24
- What is the rule for shoe loosening? Chapter 25
- What does avouch mean? Chapter 26
- What material is needed to write the laws of God upon? Chapter 27
- If you disobey God's words, the Lord will rejoice over you to? Chapter 28
- The secret things belong unto who? Chapter 29
- What is nigh unto thy mouth? Chapter 30
- Who have not known anything? Chapter 31
- Who is the Rock? Chapter 32
- Who is our refuge? Chapter 33
- Who did the Lord know face to face? Chapter 34

Joshua

- What was to be meditated day and night? Chapter 1
- In what country did the inhabitants faint? Chapter 2
- What made the ground dry? Chapter 3
- What is the memorial unto the children of Israel? Chapter 4
- Who was the captain of the Lord? Chapter 5
- Why shall Rahab the harlot lives? Chapter 6
- Why was the place called the valley of Achor? Chapter 7
- What was the great heap of stones used for? Chapter 8
- What does it mean, "make ye a league"? Chapter 9
- What was performed when the Lord hearkened unto the voice of a man? Chapter 10
- What city made peace with Israel? Chapter 11
- How many kings did the children of Israel smote? Chapter 12
- What did the Lord say to Joshua? Chapter 13
- How was the inheritance distributed? Chapter 14
- What people could the children of Judah not drive out of the land? Chapter 15
- What people could the children of Joseph not drive out of the land? Chapter 16

- What people could the children of Manasseh not drive out of the land? Chapter 17
- How many tribes did not receive their inheritance? Chapter 18
- What was the name of the land of Leshem? Chapter 19
- Why did they need cities of refuge? Chapter 20
- How many suburbs did the Levites receive? Chapter 21
- What does the altar Ed mean? Chapter 22
- What will make the Lord angry? Chapter 23
- Who outlived Joshua? Chapter 24

Judges

- The children of Benjamin did not drive out what people from Jerusalem? Chapter 1
- Why did the people weep? Chapter 2
- Who was left-handed? Chapter 3
- What was the prophetess' name? Chapter 4
- Who is the mother of Israel? Chapter 5
- Who saw an angel of the Lord face to face? Chapter 6
- How many men went to battle against the Midianites? Chapter 7
- Who ruled over the men of Israel? Chapter 8
- Why did the armourbearer kill Abimelech? Chapter 9
- What did the Lord do to Israel in his anger? Chapter 10
- Who did Jephthah offer for a burnt offering? Chapter 11
- What word could the Ephraimite not pronounce? Chapter 12
- Whose name was a secret? Chapter 13
- Who was the thirteenth Judge? Chapter 14
- From where did the water come? Chapter 15
- How did Samson lose his strength? Chapter 16
- Why did Micah believe that the Lord would do him good? Chapter 17

- Did the priest become a priest to one or a tribe? Chapter 18
- Why was the concubine divided in twelve pieces? Chapter 19
- Who went first to battle against the children of Benjamin? Chapter 20
- What tribe was cut off from Israel? Chapter 21

Ruth

- Who said, "thy God my God"? Chapter 1
- Who is the mighty man of wealth? Chapter 2
- Who is the virtuous woman? Chapter 3
- Who is the father of Jesse? Chapter 4

1 Samuel

- Who shall have no razor come upon his head? Chapter 1
- Who had favor with God and men? Chapter 2
- What was precious in those days? Chapter 3
- Why was the child named Ichabod? Chapter 4
- What relationship did the ark of the Lord have with Dagon? Chapter 5
- How many people were killed when they looked into the ark of the Lord? Chapter 6
- Who judged Israel? Chapter 7
- Why did the people want a king? Chapter 8
- What tribe is the smallest in Israel? Chapter 9
- What did the children of Belial say? Chapter 10
- How many days did the elders of Jabesh request to seek salvation? Chapter 11
- What King did Israel choose? Chapter 12
- What was Samuel's set appointed time? Chapter 13
- Who is Jonathan's father? Chapter 14
- Why was Saul rejected as king? Chapter 15
- What does God look for in a man? Chapter 16
- Who was the uncircumcised Philistine? Chapter 17
- Who was Saul's enemy? Chapter 18
- Who stripped off his clothes also? Chapter 19

- Where was the yearly sacrifice performed? Chapter 20
- What type of behavior did David display before King Achish? Chapter 21
- Who received the sword of Goliath? Chapter 22
- Who were David's men afraid of? Chapter 23
- Why did David not kill Saul? Chapter 24
- What happened to Nabal? Chapter 25
- Why did David not kill Saul? Chapter 26
- Why did David dwell in Philistine? Chapter 27
- What did Saul ask of Samuel? Chapter 28
- Why did David not fight with the Philistines? Chapter 29
- Why did the people want to stone David? Chapter 30
- Who is the house of Ashtaroth? Chapter 31

2 Samuel

- Why did David smite the stranger? Chapter 1
- Who was made king in Israel? Chapter 2
- Who are the sons of Zeruiah? Chapter 3
- Who is the lame son? Chapter 4
- What is another name for Zion? Chapter 5
- What instruments were made of wood? Chapter 6
- Did David build a house for the Lord? Chapter 7
- What did David dedicate to the Lord? Chapter 8
- Who ate at the king's table continually? Chapter 9
- What did Hanun do to David's servants? Chapter 10
- What displeased the Lord? Chapter 11
- Who was David's second child? Chapter 12
- What did Amnon do to Tamar? Chapter 13
- What is the name of Absalom's daughter? Chapter 14
- The hearts of the people follow whom? Chapter 15
- Who cursed David? Chapter 16
- Why did Ahithophel hang himself? Chapter 17
- How did Absalom die? Chapter 18
- Why did every man flee to his tent? Chapter 19
- Why did they cut off the head of Sheba? Chapter 20
- Who was the light of Israel? Chapter 21

1 Kings

- Who became king after David? Chapter 1
- Why was Joab killed? Chapter 2
- Why did Solomon speak about dividing the child? Chapter 3
- How many kings came to hear the wisdom of Solomon? Chapter 4
- Who made a league with Solomon? Chapter 5
- How many years did it take to finish building the temple? Chapter 6
- How many years did it take Solomon to finish building his house? Chapter 7
- What filled the house of the Lord? Chapter 8
- What American military did Solomon have? Chapter 9
- Whom did all the earth seek? Chapter 10
- On what city did the Lord put his name? Chapter 11
- What tribe followed the house of David? Chapter 12
- What hand did the Lord restore? Chapter 13
- Who had Sodomites in the land? Chapter 14
- Who had a disease in his foot? Chapter 15
- Who became drunk? Chapter 16
- How was Elijah fed? Chapter 17

- What did Ahab see at the sea? Chapter 18
- What did the angel do for Elijah? Chapter 19
- Who said the Lord is the God of the hills only? Chapter 20
- Who did the dogs eat? Chapter 21
- Who made their house out of ivory? Chapter 22

2 Kings

- Why did the king of Israel die? Chapter 1
- What divided the water? Chapter 2
- What was the purpose of the minstrel? Chapter 3
- How many children did the Shunammite have? Chapter 4
- From what water did Naaman receive his healing? Chapter 5
- What did the woman boil to eat? Chapter 6
- What were the windows in heaven? Chapter 7
- Who killeth Benhadad the king of Syria? Chapter 8
- Who did the dogs eat? Chapter 9
- What happened to Ahab's sons? Chapter 10
- What was the age of Jehoash when he became king? Chapter 11
- What is a breach? Chapter 12
- What happened in Elisha's sepulchre? Chapter 13
- Who became king instead of the father? Chapter 14 Who was smote with leprosy? Chapter 15
- What does "pass through the fire" mean? Chapter 16
- What secret things did the children of Israel do? Chapter 17
- What did Rabshakeh tell the children of Jerusalem? Chapter 18

- What did the angel of the Lord do? Chapter 19
- Why did Hezekiah become sick? Chapter 20
- Who shed innocent blood? Chapter 21
- What was the prophetess' name? Chapter 22
- There is no king like whom? Chapter 23
- What sin will the Lord not pardon? Chapter 24
- Who came out of prison? Chapter 25

Ezra

- Where was the house of God being built? Chapter 1
- Who could not eat of the most holy things? Chapter 2
- Who were the ancient men? Chapter 3
- Why did the work of the house of God cease? Chapter 4
- Who destroyed the latter house? Chapter 5
- What was restored? Chapter 6
- It will be unlawful to impose toll or tribute on what? Chapter 7
- Why did the Jews proclaim a fast? Chapter 8
- What was the purpose for the revival? Chapter 9
- Who was weeping before the Lord? Chapter 10

Nehemiah

- Who was the king's cupbearer? Chapter 1
- Why was Nehemiah sad? Chapter 2
- Who put not their necks to the work of their Lord? Chapter 3
- Who was feeble? Chapter 4
- Who was very angry? Chapter 5
- What prophetess tried to put fear in Nehemiah? Chapter 6
- Why was the priest removed from the priesthood? Chapter 7
- Why did the people weep? Chapter 8
- What people were sustained in the wilderness? Chapter 9
- What did the Levites do with the tithes? Chapter 10
- A certain portion of what goes to the singers. Chapter 11
- What happened in the days of David and Asaph? Chapter 12
- What curse was turned into a blessing? Chapter 13

Esther

- Who shall bear rule in their own house? Chapter 1
- What happened to Vashti? Chapter 2
- Who did not reverence Haman? Chapter 3
- Who wanted to destroy the Jews? Chapter 4
- Who spoke about hanging Mordecai? Chapter 5
- What was written in the chronicles? Chapter 6
- Who was afraid before the king and queen? Chapter 7
- What two countries had lieutenants and deputies? Chapter 8
- Who waxed greater and greater? Chapter 9
- What was written in the book of Chronicles? Chapter 10

Job

- Who was the greatest of all the men of the east? Chapter 1
- Who was considered foolish? Chapter 2
- What did I give up when I came out my mother's womb? Chapter 3
- Who became fearful and trembling? Chapter 4
- Happy is the man who God what? Chapter 5
- Teach me, and I will hold my what? Chapter 6
- What is man, that thou shouldest what? Chapter 7
- Who shall perish? Chapter 8
- He destroyeth whom? Chapter 9
- Who was confused? Chapter 10
- What is pure? Chapter 11
- Who is laughed to scorn? Chapter 12
- Though he slays me, yet will what? Chapter 13
- Who can bring a clean thing out of what? Chapter 14
- What condemneth and testifieth against me? Chapter 15
- I can shake my head at what? Chapter 16
- Who shall be stronger and stronger? Chapter 17
- What is the place of him whom knoweth not God? Chapter 18
- What can vex my soul? Chapter 19

- What is the portion of a wicked man? Chapter 20
- Depart from whom for we desire not your knowledge? Chapter 21
- He shall save what kind of person? Chapter 22
- I have esteemed the words of his mouth more than what? Chapter 23
- No eye shall see whom? Chapter 24
- Who is a worm? Chapter 25
- He hangeth the earth upon what? Chapter 26
- All the while I have breath I will not what? Chapter 27
- What is wisdom and understanding? Chapter 28
- When the secret of God was upon what? Chapter 29
- My harp and organ sound like what? Chapter 30
- I have not suffered my mouth to sin by what? Chapter 31
- Great men are not always what? Chapter 32
- The breath of the Almighty hath given me what? Chapter 33
- Who are "all are the work of his hands"? Chapter 34
- Who giveth songs in the night? Chapter 35
- How can you spend your years in prosperity and pleasures? Chapter 36
- He respecteth not whom? Chapter 37
- When his young one's cry unto God, the raven provideth what? Chapter 38
- Where does she leaveth her eggs and warmeth? Chapter 39

- What did the Lord say in the whirlwind?
  Chapter 40
- What is the deep, which boils like a pot?
  Chapter 41
- What was required of Job to receive double?
  Chapter 42

Isaiah

- The Lord delights not in what? Chapter 1
- The day of the Lord of hosts shall be upon everyone that is what? Chapter 2
- Who causes thee to err? Chapter 3
- Who shall be called holy? Chapter 4
- What has enlarged itself? Chapter 5
- Woe is who, for I am undone? Chapter 6
- What shall he eat to choose good over evil? Chapter 7
- What was the prophetess' son's name? Chapter 8
- What is the son's name? Chapter 9
- What can destroy the yoke? Chapter 10
- Who is the Branch? Chapter 11
- Who is my strength and song and salvation? Chapter 12
- "I will punish the world" for what? Chapter 13
- Who has fallen from heaven? Chapter 14
- What shall be cut off? Chapter 15
- Who is very proud? Chapter 16
- At that day shall a man look to his what? Chapter 17
- For the Lord said unto me what? Chapter 18
- Who shall fight everyone against his brother? Chapter 19

- Who was walking naked and barefoot? Chapter 20
- And he cried what? Chapter 21
- And I will fasten him as a what? Chapter 22
- What is the crowning city and the honor of the earth? Chapter 23
- Strong drink shall be bitter to them that what? Chapter 24
- Who will wipe away tears from all faces? Chapter 25
- Let favour be shewed to who? Chapter 26
- What will happen when the great trumpet sounds? Chapter 27
- How will he speak to this people? Chapter 28
- Thou shalt be visited of the Lord of hosts with what? Chapter 29
- One thousand shall flee at the rebuke of what? Chapter 30
- Now the Egyptians are men and not what? Chapter 31
- The vile person shall be no more called what? Chapter 32
- What canst thou not understand? Chapter 33
- The land shall be soaked with what? Chapter 34
- Who shall walk on the highway of holiness? Chapter 35
- Rabshakeh cried with a loud voice in what language? Chapter 36
- Who blasphemed God? Chapter 37
- The grave cannot what? Chapter 38
- What sin did Hezekiah commit? Chapter 39

- It is he that sitteth upon what of the earth? Chapter 40
- Who art thou chosen and servant? Chapter 41
- I have put my spirit upon whom? Chapter 42
- Bring forth what people that have eyes and ears? Chapter 43
- I'm the first and last and beside me there is no what? Chapter 44
- I the Lord created what things? Chapter 45
- Remember what former things of old? Chapter 46
- Who call themselves the ladies of kingdoms? Chapter 47
- There is no peace upon whom? Chapter 48
- Can a woman forget her what? Chapter 49
- I hid not my face from shame and what? Chapter 50
- Who did the Lord call alone and bless and increase? Chapter 51
- How beautiful upon the mountains are the feet of him who what? Chapter 52
- Who is despised and rejected of men? Chapter 53
- What is that formed against thee shall prosper? Chapter 54
- What shall not return unto me void? Chapter 55
- For mine house shall be called what? Chapter 56
- What spirit shall be revived? Chapter 57
- What fast is carnal? Chapter 58
- What made himself a prey? Chapter 59
- What shall you call the walls and gates? Chapter 60

- He was clothed and covered with what? Chapter 61
- What shall they call the holy people? Chapter 62
- Why were they not called by their name? Chapter 63
- What are filthy rags? Chapter 64
- "Stand by thyself and come not near me." Why? Chapter 65
- What is his throne and footstool? Chapter 66

Jeremiah

- When did the Lord know Jeremiah? Chapter 1
- Who is a home born slave? Chapter 2
- Who divorced the Lord? Chapter 3
- Where to circumcise the foreskin? Chapter 4
- The prophets prophesy what? Chapter 5
- On what paths shall they find rest? Chapter 6
- What provoked the Lord to anger? Chapter 7
- What is balm? Chapter 8
- Trust not who? Chapter 9
- He made the earth and the world and the heavens by what? Chapter 10
- Why pray not or cry for these people? Chapter 11
- If mine evil neighbors will not what, I will destroy that nation? Chapter 12
- What is good for nothing? Chapter 13
- What kinds of prophet's prophesy peace in this place? Chapter 14
- The Lord is weary with what? Chapter 15
- They will know my hand and might. What is my name? Chapter 16
- Cursed be the man who trusteth in what? Chapter 17
- Who is the clay and the potter? Chapter 18
- Who will breaketh as a potter's vessel? Chapter 19

- What was burning as fire shut up in my bones? Chapter 20

- Thus, saith the Lord, I set before you what? Chapter 21

- Woe unto him that buildeth his house by what? Chapter 22

- Who is that righteous Branch? Chapter 23

- What seeth thou, Jeremiah, what chapter? Chapter 24

- The Lord hath a controversy and pleaded with whom? Chapter 25

- Why were the people gathered against Jeremiah? Chapter 26

- Therefore, hearken not ye to your what? Chapter 27

- Why did the prophet die? Chapter 28

- What prophet was not sent from God? Chapter 29

- What did Jeremiah have to write in the book? Chapter 30

- Who did the Lord draw with loving-kindness? Chapter 31

- Thine eyes are open upon the ways of whom? Chapter 32

- What is the name of the Branch of righteousness? Chapter 33

- What happened at the end of seven years? Chapter 34

- Did the Lord command them to drink wine or not to drink wine? Chapter 35

- Did Baruch write the words of the mouth of Jeremiah with ink or a pencil? Chapter 36

- Why did Jeremiah go to prison? Chapter 37
- What did Jeremiah eat in prison? Chapter 38
- What happened to King Zedekiah? Chapter 39
- Where did Jeremiah live? Chapter 40
- Who killed Gedaliah? Chapter 41
- Who asketh Jeremiah to pray? Chapter 42
- What did the Lord command the remnant to do? Chapter 43
- How shall the remnant return back to the land of Judah? Chapter 44
- The Lord giveth thy life for a what? Chapter 45
- Thou shalt use many medicines, for thou shalt what? Chapter 46
- Why is the Lord quiet? Chapter 47
- What have we heard about Moab? Chapter 48
- What people inherit Gad? Chapter 49
- What nation refused to let Judah and Israel go? Chapter 50
- What happened when God uttered his voice? Chapter 51
- How old was Zedekiah when he reigned? Chapter 52

Ezekiel

- Who had the vision of the four living creatures? Chapter 1
- What was written on the roll? Chapter 2
- How did the roll taste? Chapter 3
- What shall be a sign to the house of Israel? Chapter 4
- Why will the remnant be scattered into all the winds? Chapter 5
- How will the remnant be spared? Chapter 6
- What information does the remnant seek from the prophet, priest, and ancients? Chapter 7
- Yet they cry loud in my ear I will what? Chapter 8
- Who says the Lord hath forsaken the earth and seeth not? Chapter 9
- What is a description of the cherubim? Chapter 10
- I will replace the stony heart with what? Chapter 11
- What will not be prolonged anymore? Chapter 12
- Woe unto who that speaketh lies? Chapter 13
- What three men were delivered by their righteousness? Chapter 14
- Who will be used for fuel? Chapter 15
- What proverb shall they use? Chapter 16
- Who is the great eagle? Chapter 17

- Does the Lord have any pleasure that the wicked should die? Chapter 18
- What is the lamentation? Chapter 19
- What is the glory of the land? Chapter 20
- Who are the righteous and the wicked? Chapter 21
- Who did the Lord find to stand in the gap? Chapter 22
- Samaria's name is Aholah and Jerusalem's name is what? Chapter 23
- Who shall be a sign unto you? Chapter 24
- What people had old hatred against the people of God? Chapter 25
- Why was judgment brought upon Tyrus? Chapter 26
- Who was in perfect beauty? Chapter 27
- Who declared themselves to be God? Chapter 28
- What people were scattered among the nations? Chapter 29
- What nation shall rebuke Egypt? Chapter 30
- Who will be cast down to hell? Chapter 31
- What nation shall be in Lamentation? Chapter 32
- I shall not remember whose iniquity or righteousness? Chapter 33
- What type of shower will come down in this season? Chapter 34
- What type of hatred does Mount Seir have against Israel? Chapter 35
- I will replace the stony heart with what? Chapter 36
- Who are the dry bones? Chapter 37

- Who shall shake at the presence of God? Chapter 38

- Who hid their faces? Chapter 39

- The vision for the son of man, behold with thine what? Chapter 40

- The temple and sanctuary have how many doors? Chapter 41

- What chamber is holy: North, South, East, or West? Chapter 42

- What is the law of the house? Chapter 43

- What can enter by the gate of the sanctuary? Chapter 44

- What size is the lot for the sanctuary? Chapter 45

- What days do the people come to worship? Chapter 46

- What should be used for medicine? Chapter 47

- How many gates are in the city? Chapter 48

Daniel

- Who stays in the king's palace from the children of Judah? Chapter 1
- Who gave the interpretation to the dream? Chapter 2
- How many people were in the fiery furnace? Chapter 3
- What happened to Nebuchadnezzar's pride? Chapter 4
- What happened to Belshazzar's pride? Chapter 5
- What happened to Daniel in the lion's den? Chapter 6
- Who is the Ancient of days? Chapter 7
- What is the vision of the ram and the rough goat? Chapter 8
- Who was flying and touched Daniel? Chapter 9
- Who is Michael the chief prince? Chapter 10
- What are flatteries? Chapter 11
- What words are closed that Daniel understood not? Chapter 12

Hosea

- How many children did Hosea have? Chapter 1
- Thou shall call me what and call me no more Baali? Chapter 2
- How much did Hosea pay for his wife? Chapter 3
- My people are destroyed for lack of what? Chapter 4
- Who will return to their place? Chapter 5
- What does the Lord desire more than? Chapter 6
- Strangers have made their hair what? Chapter 7
- They have sown what and reap what? Chapter 8
- O Lord what will thou give them? Chapter 9
- Break up your what ground? Chapter 10
- Why will the Lord not destroy Ephraim? Chapter 11
- Who shall leave his blood upon him? Chapter 12
- What happened in Samaria? Chapter 13
- Ye are our gods: who or what? Chapter 14

Joel

- What did the people do when they gathered themselves? Chapter 1
- What happens when the spirit pours upon all flesh? Chapter 2
- I will sell your sons and your daughters to whom? Chapter 3

Amos

- What nations had transgressions against the Lord? Chapter 1
- Who sold the poor for a pair of shoes? Chapter 2
- How can two walks unless they do what? Chapter 3
- What is God's name? Chapter 4
- Why will the Lord not hear the noise of their songs? Chapter 5
- How was the house of Israel at ease? Chapter 6
- What did Amaziah the priest charge Amos to do? Chapter 7
- What famine did the Lord send to the land? Chapter 8
- Who is called by his name? Chapter 9

Obadiah

- Who shall judge the Mount of Esau? Chapter 1

Jonah

- What swallowed up Jonah? Chapter 1
- What happened to Jonah after he prayed? Chapter 2
- To whom did Jonah preach? Chapter 3
- Why was Jonah angry? Chapter 4

Micah

- What is incurable? Chapter 1
- Why can he be the prophet to this people? Chapter 2
- What do the judge, the priests, and the prophets have in common? Chapter 3
- What shall be beaten into the plowshares? Chapter 4
- Who is little among the thousands of Judah? Chapter 5
- With what will the Lord be pleased? Chapter 6
- Trust ye not in a what? Chapter 7

Nahum

- The Lord is slow to what? Chapter 1
- What is old like a pool of water? Chapter 2
- Why was Nineveh judged? Chapter 3

Habakkuk

- What burden did Habakkuk see? Chapter 1
- The just shall live by what? Chapter 2
- The Lord will make my feet like what? Chapter 3

Zephaniah

- What shall not be able to deliver them from the Lord's wrath? Chapter 1
- To what nations shall the Lord bring judgment? Chapter 2
- What types of people will trust in the Lord? Chapter 3

Haggai

Zechariah

- The angel who communed with Zechariah said what? Chapter 1
- Who is the apple of his eye? Chapter 2
- Who is the Branch? Chapter 3
- Not by might, nor by power, but by what? Chapter 4
- What was written in the flying roll? Chapter 5
- What colors are the four chariots? Chapter 6
- What type of heart, that they should not hear the law? Chapter 7
- What city is called, the city of truth? Chapter 8
- Who is riding upon an ass? Chapter 9
- Who will walk up and down in the name of the Lord? Chapter 10
- Who bought thirty pieces of silver? Chapter 11
- I will destroy all the nations that come against whom? Chapter 12
- Who had wounds in their hands? Chapter 13
- There shall be one Lord and his name is what? Chapter 14

Malachi

- My name shall be great among what? Chapter 1
- Have we not one father and one what? Chapter 2
- Can a man rob God: yes, or no? Chapter 3
- Who will come to turn the heart of man? Chapter 4

NOTES

NOTES

NOTES

www.ingramcontent.com/pod-product-compliance
Lightning Source LLC
Chambersburg PA
CBHW051242120626
46547CB00014B/1763